BIRCH
BOOKS

First published by Birch Books 2024

Copyrights - Insert Actual Author Name

All rights reserved

ISBN 978-81-969746-9-5

All rights reserved. No part of this publication may be reproduced, stored in a retrieval system or transmitted in any form or by any means, electronic, mechanical, photocopying, recording or otherwise, without the prior permission of the author.

 birch.books

www.birchbooks.in

To all those littles who need a bit more time and faith and kindness than everybody else.
~ Mithila Karnik-Adarkar

To everybody who is having a hard time coming into their own. It is not the destination but the journey.
~ Prerana Manker

Was very shy but very sweet...

2.

She watched her siblings tickle some toes...

She stole a glance at the lazy ones...

5.

She was scared to splash her way to the shore...

9.

She thought the sand would make her sore...

She thought she wouldn't be as good as them...

Her friends ignored her as they came and went...

12.

She felt alone, she wished she was...

But then one day, a little girl...

Swam to her and did a twirl...

16.

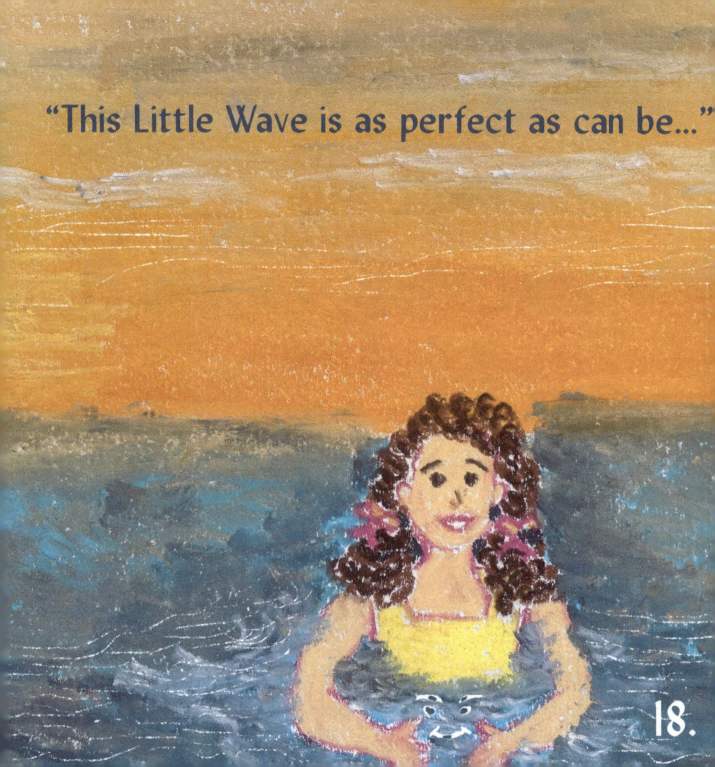

To feel good and become brave.

Sometimes it takes a roll of your tongue
Like Cerulean or Admiral

25.

27. Do you feel like dipping in Sapphire
Put all those toes out of line...?

Are some waves Lapis and some Navy,
Just like some are calm or extra wavy?

28.

I am Prussian, I am Aquamarine,
I am the Sea, I am of the Blues.

Printed in the USA
CPSIA information can be obtained
at www.ICGtesting.com
LVHW060933091224
798491LV00006B/131